my name is

Pamela Jean

A Story of Abortion as Seen through the Eyes of a Child

Thank you John for your support and honor for my husband.

Debra Denise Watkins, M.Ed., PhD

Debbie Watkins

"The Chief's Wife."

July 16, 2021

My Name is Pamela Jean:
A Story of Abortion as Seen through the Eyes of a Child
By Debra Denise Watkins, M.Ed., PhD
Copyright 2019 © All rights reserved.

Unless otherwise noted, all Scripture quotations are taken from The Living Bible copyright © 1971. Used by permission of Tyndale House Publishers, Inc., Carol Stream, Illinois 60188. All rights reserved.

Scripture quotations marked (NIV) are taken from the Holy Bible, New International Version®, NIV®. Copyright © 1973, 1978, 1984, 2011 by Biblica, Inc.™ Used by permission of Zondervan. All rights reserved worldwide. www.zondervan.com The "NIV" and "New International Version" are trademarks registered in the United States Patent and Trademark Office by Biblica, Inc.™

Scripture quotations marked (KJV) are taken from the Holy Bible, King James Version (Public Domain).

Scripture quotations marked (NABRE) are taken from the New American Bible, revised edition © 2010, 1991, 1986, 1970 Confraternity of Christian Doctrine, Inc., Washington, DC All Rights Reserved.

ISBN: 978-0-578-58659-5

Cover and Book Design by Exodus Design
www.ExodusDesign.com

Defend the Innocent
Houston, TX USA

Be fearless in your stand for truth and honesty. And may God use you to defend the innocent (2 Chronicles 19:11).

Table *of* Contents

My Story

"From my mother's womb, You have been my God."
Psalm 22:10

Choices of Destiny

Miracles at the Crossroads of Life

Acknowledgement

This book seeks to acknowledge, honor, and bring praise to the Creator of life and the Father of all mankind. Despite our complicity with those things that have separated us from His purpose and plans for our lives, it is possible to rise from the ashes of our past and begin again.

May we acknowledge that every breath and every beating pulse of our heart is a gift of love and grace. May these seeds of grace bring healing, hope, and restoration to those who have been destroyed and torn apart by their participation in the destruction of life through abortion. And for those who stand at the threshold of destiny, may God give you the courage to say "yes" to the life that God himself has knit together in the first home your child will ever know.

May the God of all grace and mercy give each heart and mind the peace of God that passes all understanding as we become the voice for the unborn, the humble champions for life, and the grateful recipients of a Father's forever forgiveness, love, and care.

To Him be glory, both now and forever more.

A Child's *Dedication* for Life

This book is dedicated to the millions of children who have never had an Earth birthday, just like me, but who are seated now in the throne room of God— forever loved, forever known, and forever in the arms of God.

With all my love,
Pamela Jean

Blue Eyes

My eyes are blue.
Shining bright,
I look a lot like you.

I think you would have loved me,
I really have true worth.
It's hard to believe
That one simple choice
Could have given me my birth.

In heaven, where I now abide,
Some say I am beautiful.
And once again I hear some say,
"I look so much like you."
And if there were tears in heaven,
Tears would freely flow
From my innocent eyes of blue.

So Mom, I have only one question
Crying out within my heart.
Why did one choice on Earth
Stop my beating heart?

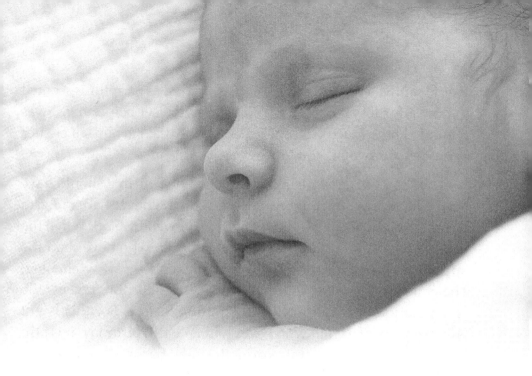

From the $\mathcal{A}uthor's$ Heart

This story was birthed in my heart during a visit to one of our local pregnancy centers. The director of the center gave me a tour and explained the purpose of each room in the center. When the director and I walked into the ultrasound room, I was shown small replicas of a baby's development from conception to birth. My heart was deeply and profoundly touched by the images presented to me in this room. I saw with renewed clarity the value of life created by God himself.

That same evening, I sat down at my desk and began to write. It was as if the very words that were being transcribed from my heart were coming from a little girl who never had an Earth birthday, but whose heart and life still had a very real story to tell.

As Pamela Jean's story began to unfold, this beautiful child's words captivated my heart. I was also amazed as Scriptures seemed to flow effortlessly onto the pages that were set before me. I was reminded how much God cherishes the life that He himself creates in the sanctuary of a mother's womb.

The story of Pamela Jean is a reflection of a life that should have been. She represents millions of children who never had an Earth birthday, but who are forever known and loved by God. When the reality of abortion is faced, stories of children who never had the opportunity to reach their full potential can be heart wrenching. The child in this story, and in all stories of abortion, reveals the victimization of the most helpless in our society. For this is not only the story of a child who never had an Earth birthday, it is also the story of a nation and world that has become complicit in creating the stage for the most significant holocaust of human life in history.

When a child is lost through death, we grieve. This sorrow, however, becomes greater when a child's life could have been saved through a simple act of a mother's decision to choose life.

Based on the truths of God's Word, this book provides inspiration and hope for women, of all ages and from all walks of life, who stand at the threshold of destiny and choice. For women who feel compelled to choose between the life of their child or an abortion, this book provides inspiration to choose life over death.

For those who have had an abortion, Pamela Jean's story reveals God's incredible mercy and love for women who have found themselves trapped in Satan's web of deceit.

And finally, for men and women who work daily to defend life, this book can be used as a tool to communicate the value of a child's life directly from the words spoken by a beautiful little girl known and loved by God himself.

May Pamela Jean's tender voice give us wisdom to face our personal and corporate fears, rejections, and heartbreaks with faith as we remember the lives of countless children who should have been.

May the wisdom of God's word intertwined within this story give us the courage to stand for truth and life for the children whose hearts still cry out to us for both mercy and love.

And finally, may the words of a little girl who never had an Earth birthday make us mindful always of the worth, value, and beauty of God's most beautiful and sacred gifts to mankind...our children.

Foreword

*"A voice was heard in Ramah, sobbing and loud lamentation;
Rachel weeping for her children, and she would not be consoled,
since they were no more."*
Matthew 2:18[1]

The first lie the enemy tells a woman in a crisis pregnancy is that the baby she is carrying is just a "blob" of tissues. This woman is like an animal with its paw caught in a trap; it will chew off the paw to free itself. Initially, when a woman walks out of an abortion clinic, she oftentimes feels a sense of relief; her "problem" has been solved.

Sadly, I was one of those women over 43 years ago. Nagging me in the back of my subconscious was the realization that what I had done was wrong. The doctor who performed the procedure never looked at me or said one word to me. I felt like he knew in his heart that what we were both doing was wrong. My husband and I confessed our sin within a very short time.

You see, a woman's body was made by God to be fruitful and bear new life. When God's beautiful plan is destroyed, it resonates in our souls. It is heartbreaking that one out of every three women have walked this sad path.

For over 20 years I suffered with post-abortion syndrome. I confessed and confessed my sin, but I did not, and could not believe that God would forgive me. I felt unworthy of His love and could not forgive myself. I was always waiting for God's vengeance to strike me. I feared that He would take one of my

XI

beautiful three children to punish me. Twenty years ago a pastor said to me, "You need to forgive yourself. Your baby in heaven forgives you and is praying that you forgive yourself."

This was the first time anyone had ever referred to my "abortion" as a "baby." It took my breath away! It had been too painful to think of my baby as a baby. I knew I needed help and healing. God led me to a post-abortion Bible study where I learned the true character of God. He was waiting with open arms to embrace and forgive His prodigal daughter. I learned through my study with other post-abortive women to forgive myself and to forgive those who had betrayed me. I truly was, as Debra Watkins says in her book, "a new creation."

I was blessed to meet Debra at the beginning of her journey as she was laboring to give birth to this precious book. Debra's visit to a local crisis pregnancy center was truly ordained by God. I know that Debra will touch the hearts of many in giving voice to the "known by God, and loved by God," Pamela Jean.

Debra destroys the enemy's lie that His creation is a "blob" of tissue. God's creation has a face and a name, and in this book, it is Pamela Jean. It breaks my heart to think of all the millions of nameless babies sitting next to the throne of God. Along with all the nameless babies, there are millions of nameless women and men who have bought into the enemy's lie.

Debra Watkins's precious Pamela Jean will open the hearts of those who are hurting from their abortion. Through this sweet story of the child who never had an Earth birthday, mothers will be able to embrace and learn to love the precious gift that God has entrusted to them.

Debra gives us a path to see how God can take what the enemy meant for evil and turn it into good! Those hurting from abortion will learn, too, that our God is a forgiving Father who loves us beyond measure, and most poignantly that our precious, much-loved-by-God, children are waiting to embrace us in heaven for all of eternity. As Debra says, "Death has no victory when God is in control!"

Most importantly, Debra Watkins's book is a treasure that, with God's grace, will "provide inspiration for young women who stand at the threshold of destiny and choice."

"I call heaven and Earth to witness against you that today I have set before you life or death, blessing or curse. Oh, that you would choose life, that you and your children might live!" (Deut. 30:19)

Karen Perez
Silent No More Regional Coordinator – Houston, Texas
Houston Coalition for Life
Founding and Current Board of Directors

A Day of Destiny

"I call heaven and Earth to witness against you that today I have set before you life or death, blessing or curse. Oh, that you would choose life that you and your children might live!"
Deuteronomy 30:19

She waited outside of a room that no one would have counted as a model of modernity or cleanliness. She wondered how she ever became part of such an unusual scene. A few mismatched chairs and an outdated calendar on the wall left the impression that this was a room that had not garnered any thought, attention, or careful planning. The sparse furnishings and unkempt conditions seemed to be in harmony with those who were seemingly gathered for this event of unparalleled significance.

Faces of destiny were reflected in each guest who had been slated to participate in this unprecedented day of choice. Some appeared happy and glad to be attending; others seemed distant and alone. Still, others who had gathered in this room seemed to be careless reflections of a society that had abandoned them many years before this fateful day.

Reflective of the times, a young couple from a counter culture where rules were meant for everyone but themselves, was sitting side by side with a gleeful look of anticipation on their faces, as if some grand and glorious event was about to occur. There was also a young girl waiting with her mother, probably no more than 12 years old, who obviously was one of the youngest clients in the room. Then there she sat, a young and somewhat impressionable college student completely immune to the reality of what was about to happen.

Despite the differences of age and perception of those sitting in this room, it is certain that the angels in heaven cried. God himself was also watching with a broken heart as this incredible drama of both life and death began to unfold.

On this day, three new souls would enter heaven's gates. The lives of the couple, the mother and her 12-year-old child, and the young college student would be forever changed. For even though society's own laws supported the happenings in this room, there is no denying that on this day, three beautiful children entered the gates of heaven—too early and too soon.

The consequences of this type of decision are eternal. Were it not for the Father of Life intervening, all hope for future reconciliation would have been forever lost. However, because the Father of Life is also the God of all Mercy, a plan to offer forgiveness, hope, and a new beginning was already in place.

Today if you are in your own room of destiny, seek God's will and heart. When the choice to be made reflects the sanctity of life, choose life that you and your child may live.

Chapter 1

My Name is Pamela Jean

A Child, Not a Choice

I have always been a child, not just a choice.

All my love,

Pamela Jean

My Father's *Plan* for Me

"You saw me before I was born and scheduled each day of my life
before I began to breathe. Every day was recorded in your Book!
How precious it is, Lord, to realize that you are thinking
about me constantly.

I can't even count how many times a day
your thoughts turn towards me!
And when I waken in the morning,
you are still thinking of me."
Psalm 139:16-18

My name is Pamela Jean. I am known by God and loved by God. I am beautiful and without blemish. I am as perfect as the glittering stars in the nighttime sky. I am as radiant as the sunbeams lighting the day, for "I am fearfully and wonderfully made."[2] It is an amazing thing to think about. Even the very hairs on my head are numbered.[3]

My Father knew me before I was formed in my mother's womb; He sanctified me and appointed me as His spokesman to the world.[4] Therefore, I will praise Him forever for loving me and making me part of His family.

My name, Pamela Jean, the name that God gave me before the

day I was to have been born, springs forth with life and reminds me that God created me to be like a beautiful fragrance filling the incredible expanse of God's kingdom where I now abide. When someone calls out to me, I am forever mindful that even my name reflects God's glory and means "God is Gracious."

In heaven I have learned that God had a plan for my life before the foundations of the world ever existed. When He formed me in my mother's womb, He had already set apart my life to honor and glorify Him throughout all eternity.[5] God himself knit me together and was so excited about my grand entrance into the world that He gathered the angels around His throne just to celebrate my birth.[6]

But I never had an Earth birthday. Before I was ever cradled in the arms of my mother or saw the first sunrise of a beautiful summer day, my life was taken away. Even though my mother did not give birth to me on Earth, my heavenly Father took what the enemy meant as evil and turned it around for my good.

I felt a tear in my eye when I first left the beautiful sanctuary of life God had created for me in my mother's womb, but my sadness did not last long. My wonderful, heavenly Father washed away my tears.[7]

I soon discovered there is no sorrow or mourning in heaven, as the joy of the Lord fills the sky.[8] Instead, there is dancing and singing around God's throne. For I know that I was created in the image of God himself, and even in heaven I have a purpose to declare the wonderful things "God has ready for those who love the Lord."[9] And I do love my Father with all my heart.

I love my mother, too, even though I have never felt the soft touch of her hand on mine or heard her sing a mother's lullaby. I can love my mother because my Father has made me complete in Him. I can forgive her and love her with the same type of love my Father has shown to me and others who are seated near the heavenly throne of God.

 Talk

1. How does the story of Pamela Jean remind us that children created in the very image of God have life, value, and purpose?

_____

_____

_____

_____

_____

_____

2. Does the story of a little girl who never had an Earth birthday help us to understand the realities and consequences of life choices regarding the sanctity of life?

_____

_____

_____

_____

_____

Chapter 2

I'm Destiny's Child

Still a Child of Destiny

Even though I was rejected at birth,
I am still a child of destiny
because of my Father's great love for me.

Forever grateful,

Pamela Jean

Rejected at Birth

Rejected at birth
How can it be?
No mother to hold me,
No life to see.

But while forsaken
And forgotten on Earth,
The Lord Himself
Gave me a heavenly birth.

So now I can sing
A sweet simple song,
God's love is great,
To Him I belong.

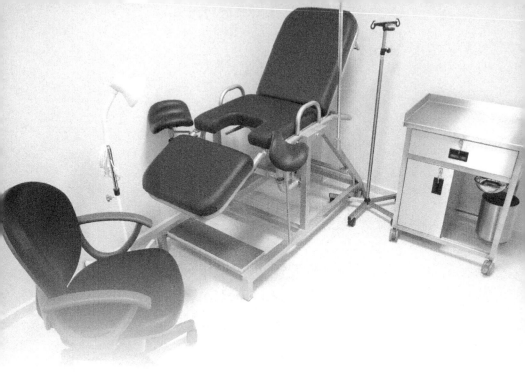

My mother was sent home from the chaotic rooms of the abortion clinic as if nothing had happened. But she knew in her heart, too late, that her decision was one that she would have to live with the rest of her life and that this decision would affect generations to come.

But even at the very moment I was rejected on Earth, the gates of heaven opened wide, for heaven is made up of children just like me. Thousands of children who never had an Earth birthday began to sing songs of love that were so beautiful and rare, it was hard to imagine that they were singing for me and welcoming me to my new heavenly home.

There is nothing on Earth that I know of that could compare to the beautiful words and music that greeted me at heaven's gate. After seeing heaven for myself, I know that no eyes on Earth have seen or ears have even heard the wonderful things God has in store for those who love Him.[10]

On the day I entered heaven, I had to go through a beautiful door. It opened wide for me, for there was a cross at the entrance that pointed the way I should go. There is no darkness here in heaven. This is because God himself is light.[11] God's light shines so bright that here we do not need the sun or moon, for His presence fills all of His creation with the majestic glow of His glory and grace.

My new home is beautiful too. It is an everlasting home that can never be taken away from me.[12] My mother's eyes have never viewed the beauty that I see now, but someday she will see the glories of heaven. What joys we will share! Here the streets are pure gold[13] and are "filled with boys and girls at play."[14]

We sometimes sit around and talk of how things might have been, but we are quick to forget the past and look forward to what lies ahead.[15] And what wondrous things they are! The beauty and warmth of His love shines throughout the heavens and fills every corner of the sky.[16] God himself surrounds us every day with His own kindness, peace, and joy.[17]

There is nothing here that we need. We are never thirsty, for His well of living water bursts forth in trickling springs and refreshes us daily beside quiet streams.[18] Because we are so loved by the Father, He daily helps us and guides us to "do what honors Him the most."[19]

I never had a home on Earth I could call my own, but here in heaven I have a beautiful house God has made just for me. On Earth I hear this house would be called a mansion, but here we just call our houses home.[20]

 Talk

1. Each time a child loses his or life on the battlefield of choice, the potential of a newborn human being is lost forever. How does this reality impact your viewpoint regarding the dignity and rights of the unborn child?

_____

_____

_____

_____

_____

_____

2. What lessons can you glean from this chapter about the value and worth of children in and outside of a mother's womb?

_____

_____

_____

_____

_____

Chapter 3

A Child Without A Choice

A Question of Rights

Where were my rights on the day I was to have been born?

Worthy of life,

Pamela Jean

If I Could Choose

If I could choose
For just one moment in time,
I would choose to live life
With your hand in mine.

But since this time on Earth
For me, can never be,
I pray that another mother's choice
Will give her child a destiny.

In heaven, there are many children here just like me. We are not unworthy or unloved, for we have been created in the image of God himself. Although I was rejected on Earth, the gates of heaven opened wide for me on the day I left the very womb of protection God had designed just for me.

The angels knew just what to do upon my early arrival. You see, even though I was rejected on Earth, the hosts of heaven knew that I was a masterpiece of my Father's love and care. For this reason, God gets the glory for everything—even when Earth's decisions take us far away from His plan and purpose for our lives.[21]

I can see from the windows of heaven that every day of my life had been written in God's book since the beginning of time. God's perfect plan was for me to have life and to have it more abundantly. But through choices other than my own, the life on Earth that was planned for me slipped away in the twinkling of an eye.

Only God can take death and turn it into life, and now in heaven He is going to use my life to show others how perfect the Father's plan is for every child He creates. I now know that everything, both in heaven and on Earth, can work together for good when God is in control.[22] Because of my story, many will come to know my Father and to trust Him now more than ever because of all that He has done for me.

 Talk

1. If you are ever faced with an unplanned pregnancy, how can you go forward with confidence, assurance, and faith?

_____

_____

_____

_____

_____

_____

2. How can your faith help to sustain you in this season of decision and choice?

_____

_____

_____

_____

_____

_____

_____

Chapter 4

My Father has Silenced the Enemy

I Am a *Reflection* of My Father's Love

My Father has silenced the enemy.

I was not a mistake.

In the eyes of heaven,

I am a remarkable reflection

of my Father's love and care for me

all the days of my life.

Amazed by His grace–

Overwhelmed by His love,

Pamela Jean

A Father's *Word* for an Overcoming Life

"The thief's purpose is to steal, kill, and destroy.
My purpose is to give life in all its fullness."
John 10:10

Mom, I *Know* He Gave You His Life

There is hope for tomorrow,

When faith lives today,

Because the Lord, our Father,

Has made you a way —

To find new beginnings,

You are bought with a price,

Mom, He loved you so much,

He gave you His life!

With all my love,

Pamela Jean

There is one thing that Earth has that heaven does not, the enemy. My Father was not surprised about my early entrance into heaven. God sent His Son to Earth thousands of years before I came on the scene. It seemed as if He died too early, just like me. However, death has never stopped my Father from accomplishing His grand plans and design for the children of men.

Evil men took His Son and nailed Him to a cross. It was not hatred that held Christ on the cross; it was love. On the third day, God raised Jesus from the grave. He made a way for us to enter into the glorious riches of His forgiveness and grace.

God's love and light are always stronger than the darkness of night and hate. In my Father's house, the glory of His presence fills the skies of heaven with joy and delight. There is no room for sadness or sorrow here because the light of His countenance shines down upon each one of His children who dance across the skies of heaven singing and delighting themselves in the goodness and mercy of the Lord.

Death has no victory when God is in control.[23] He has conquered the grave. That's why, even in death, my Father is always in control, and everything will work together for His good.[24] From the very moment I was created, God was not only watching after me, He was also watching out for my mother as well.

I know this because the moment my mother realized I was truly a gift from my Father, I saw a tear fall from her eye. I heard her calling my name to come back. But it was too late. Yet, while my mother's heart was breaking, in less than a twinkling of an eye, I was in the presence of my Father, my place of perfect peace and refuge.

What joy I felt when I heard my Father calling out my name. Even the angels welcomed me to my new heavenly home. I was not unwanted or unloved, for a thousand rays of sunlight beamed from heaven's skies.

But just like my Father is surrounded by a host of heavenly angels, the enemy is surrounded by those who serve him with wicked intentions and hate. They delighted when my mother placed me on the altar of choice. This was the day that I was forever separated on Earth from those He had created to love me and care for me all the days of my life.

My mother listened to those who said my life did not exist. Then, within a moment in time, my beating heart stopped. The enemy rejoiced. He was sure my mother's eternal fate was sealed. He moved on victoriously to find new souls who could easily be made to walk away from their first love.[25]

My mother was deeply wounded by the enemy. At times it seemed she was hopeless and all alone. I had been taken away from her too soon, and because of this, her own heart was breaking and longing for a place of redemption and hope.

My mother's sorrow touched the very throne room of God, for my Father never despises a broken and contrite heart.[26] He was waiting with arms open wide and ready to forgive. He not only forgave my mother for where she had been and what she had done, He also gave her a new life where old things have passed away and all things have become new.[27] God even showed my mother that He still has a plan for her life—a plan that is full of forgiveness and love.[28]

My Father has given my mother a brand new life. The new life that has sprung forth in my mother's heart is nothing short of a miracle. She no longer feels empty and alone, for Christ has given her new hope and an assurance that He will always be with her now and forevermore.[29]

 Talk

1. Abortion stops the beating heart of a child. Why do you think many in society still believe that a woman has the right to choose between life or death?

_____

_____

_____

_____

_____

_____

2. God offers hope to anyone who is of a broken and contrite heart. Have you experienced God's new life and forgiveness as your own?

_____

_____

_____

_____

_____

_____

Chapter 5

More Valuable than Sparrows

$\mathcal{H}e$ is Everything to Me

The enemy declared to the world that I was nothing,

but my Father stepped in and claimed me as His own.

Now He is everything to me.

With a grateful heart,

Pamela Jean

Two for a Penny

*"Not one sparrow (What do they cost? Two for a penny?)
can fall to the ground without your Father knowing it.
And the very hairs of your head are all numbered.
So, don't worry!
You are more valuable to Him than many sparrows."*
Matthew 10:29-31

God Sees *Each* Sparrow Fall

God sees each place a sparrow falls
So I know that He can see,
The sadness of a mother's heart
When she gives up a child like me.

Two for a penny,
Not valuable to some,
But for children just like me
That's why God sent His Son.

45

In God's forever plan, children are miracles, direct from the Father's heart and hand. As soon as my mother was told she was carrying a child, God knew she was carrying me! My own joy knew no end.

From the very beginning of my life, God was making me who He wanted me to be. Within a few short weeks my heart was already beating, and I started turning circles in my temporary home just from the sheer joy of being alive. I never would have imagined that the joy I was feeling for life would be taken away from me in such a short period of time.

My mother was told that I had no purpose or life, so in heaven, God had to dry my tears for He knew that on Earth His will for me would never be. There are times, even now, when I close my eyes and imagine what it would have been like to live on Earth.

When I see the sparrows in heaven's beautiful sky, I am often reminded of the incredible love my Father has for me. Sparrows, just like me, seem small and insignificant. But my Father knows when even the tiniest of these sparrows fall, so I know that He is always watching over me.

Although my birth was not welcomed on Earth, my Father has never stopped loving me. My life is a reminder that when God creates a life, the child knit together in a mother's womb will be alive forevermore on Earth and in heaven. For this reason, I know that God will use my story to help others know that when God creates a child, He creates a miracle. And for my mother, the miracle He created was me.

 Talk

1. When a child's life and potential is lost through the act of abortion, heaven must shed many tears. Have you shed tears over a past decision that you or someone you know has made regarding the lost promises and destiny of a child who never had an Earth birthday?

_____

_____

_____

_____

_____

2. How has this experience impacted your views and convictions regarding the sanctity of life?

_____

_____

_____

_____

_____

_____

Chapter 6

A New Beginning

Amazing Grace

My Father is amazing!

He has given my mother a new beginning

and a new start.

With a grateful heart,

Pamela Jean

New Beginnings

"When someone becomes a Christian,
he becomes a brand new person inside.
He is not the same anymore.
A new life has begun!"
2 Corinthians 5:17

You're a Child of the King

"In Christ, you are His child. You are raised up with Him. You are forgiven. Even now, God is holding your child close. And in Christ, you will be reunited in love."[30]
Francine Rivers

I am glad to report that my mother is a miracle.[31] She is a new creation, just like me! I have stood with a great cloud of witnesses watching my mother's progress.[32] She is amazing!

I can see her tears from heaven, and I have seen how God is washing away the past and giving her new hope and courage to go forward in the new life He has planned for her since the beginning of time.

For the sadness my mother has experienced, God has given her joy. God has swept away the ashes of my mother's regrets and given her a new beauty and peace that only He could give. She is now like a graceful oak standing strong and beautiful for the Lord's glory and use in His Kingdom.[33] She is laying aside every weight[34] that once held her captive to the enemy, and she is now going forward with my Father's plan for her life.

My Father loves her so much and only wants the best for her. She is finally realizing that God is her Father, too, and that He truly loves her and wants to give her a full and abundant life.[35] I can see more and more every day that my mother is growing in wisdom and grace. God has created in her a new heart full of life and hope. Her joy knows no end![36]

The enemy tried to destroy my mother's life, but God stepped in and changed her life forever. She is now storing up rich treasures in heaven because she is living by faith and not by sight, for she has stopped looking at the past, and is now looking forward to everything my heavenly Father has planned for her, today and forevermore.[37]

I often hear my mother's prayers reaching out to my Father for His help in the life that she is now living for His glory on Earth. God has answered her prayers by giving her joy for sorrow, laughter for tears, and new hope for despair because of my Father's great love and care for her.

I am pleased to say that my mother is becoming more like my

Father every day. She is using her life to tell others about the incredible things He is doing in her life, and how her life has been made completely new.

My heavenly Father not only gave my mother a new life, but he also gave her someone to love—someone who would stand beside her and love her in a way that only God could have planned. She is loved now both in heaven and on Earth, and has a beautiful purpose for living. Her joy shines brightly for all to see.[38]

Life Talk

1. Communicating with your Father is an important part of developing a close and lasting relationship with the One who loves you and wants the best for you. Is there a prayer you would like to share with your heavenly Father to guide and direct you in this "season of choice?"

_____

_____

_____

_____

_____

2. You are loved and valued by God himself. How can acting upon this truth change your heart and life forever?

_____

_____

_____

_____

_____

Chapter 7

Beauty for Ashes

Reflecting *His* Glory

"To all who mourn in Israel he will give beauty for ashes,
joy instead of mourning, praise instead of heaviness.
For God has planted them like strong and graceful oaks
for His own glory."
Isaiah 61:3

A Storehouse of Treasures

My Father has a rich
storehouse of treasures
where He gives beauty for ashes,
a new life for the old,
and a hope for tomorrow
that will never grow old.

Amazed by His love,

Pamela Jean

I think my mother is beautiful. God made her that way. It's a different kind of beauty that only God can give; it comes from the boundless grace of my heavenly Father. Satan had tried to destroy her life, but God has turned her around for His good and glory. Someday very soon I will see my mother for the first time face to face, and we can celebrate everything that God has done in her life and in mine. What a beautiful day this will be!

Her beauty is growing inwardly as her life begins to reflect Christ's magnificent love and care for her. She is like a light on a hill shining beautifully for all the world to see.[39] The light that she is giving to others is now helping many who have also lost their way.

She gives my Father glory for everything in her life. She knows that because of Him she has a peace that passes all understanding—even when the way is not easy, and her burdens are hard to bear.[40]

My mother has asked God to create in her a pure heart and to renew a steadfast spirit within her life.[41] God has answered her prayer by saying that though her sins were like scarlet, they would now be as clean as freshly fallen snow and as white as wool.[42] My Father has not only given my mother a beautiful and pure heart overflowing with the Father's love,[43] He has also given her a new purpose in life.

God has even given her back the years the locusts destroyed.[44] Every day I see her "youth renewed like the eagles."[45] My heavenly Father has given her "beauty instead of ashes, joy instead of mourning, and a garment of praise instead of a spirit of despair."[46] Her beauty is growing every day, and this beauty can never be taken away.

Talk

1. How can the promises of God inspire a woman who is at the crossroads of decision to make good and godly choices?

_____

_____

_____

_____

_____

_____

_____

2. When God restores a woman's heart, He can give her beauty for ashes. What does this mean in your own life today?

_____

_____

_____

_____

_____

Chapter 8

Mother-Daughter Talk:
God Blessed Me When He Gave Me You

To My *Mother*

I looked through the pages in my Father's Book of Life,
and I saw your name beautifully written
with the crimson red ink of His love.

With a heart full of praise,

Pamela Jean

Crimson Red:
My Mother's Song of Hope

Lord, I have looked inside my heart.

It is stained with crimson red.

I cannot take the guilt away,

Of this color, crimson red.

But you said to me so clearly,

Child, remember who I am.

I can make you clean again;

This has always been My plan.

So, Lord, can you forgive me?

My sin is deep within.

I am trusting in your promises,

In faith, to begin again.

$\mathcal{M}om$, Did You Know?

"I have never stopped thanking God for you.
I pray for you constantly, asking God, the glorious Father
of our Lord Jesus Christ, to give you wisdom
to see clearly and really understand who Christ is
and all that He has done for you."
Ephesians 1:16 -17

The angels told me I should say a word to my mother, so Mom, this part of my story is for you! From the first breath of life that was given to me when the miracle of life began, I knew that I would love you forever.

I did not understand why my life was taken from me before I could make my grand entrance into the world. But while I was still deep inside your womb, my Father watched with tear-filled eyes as He saw my life being torn apart from yours. He had given you me, even though you had walked away from His will and purpose for your life. But I know, from the Father's heart to mine, I would have been one of God's richest blessings in your life.

Even though you did not understand that I was bustling forth with life in your womb, I still love you with my whole heart. But we can stop looking at the things that are behind us and begin looking forward to the wonderful things God still has in store for your life and for mine.

I know from the very words of my Father that you are loved beyond measure. Our Father wants you to grow in grace and in the love of the Lord. You are the apple of God's eye![47] The more you learn to love Him on Earth, the more glorious your praise will be for Him in heaven. He loves you more than you will ever know, and He loves me too.

I remember the day when I heard you calling out my Father's name. Your heart was so broken, it made me cry too, but this was the day my Father wrote your name in His incredible Book of Life. Songs of rejoicing were everywhere. I heard the music in heaven myself.

It was quite a celebration. The whole hosts of heaven burst forth into song. Another child of God had come home. I even danced around God's throne when I heard about the wonderful things my Father was doing in your life. I loved you then, and I love you now. God blessed me when He gave me you.

Talk

1. When God gives the gift of life, He is also creating a child that will be joined to a mother's heart and life forever. If you have life now growing within you, how can the love of your child encourage you to respect and honor the sanctity of life?

_____

_____

_____

_____

_____

2. As a woman of God, you can know that You are a new creation in Christ and are beautiful because you reflect Your Father's image. How can this new knowledge inspire hope, healing, and restoration?

_____

_____

_____

_____

_____

Chapter 9

My Father's Plan for You

My Heart is *Glad*

Even though I never had an Earth birthday,
my heart is glad because I know that God has
incredible things in store for your life.
He already knows the plans He has for you.

Your daughter,

Pamela Jean

Your *Future* is in God's Hand

"For I know the plans I have for you," says the Lord.
"They are plans for good and not for evil,
to give you a future and a hope."
Jeremiah 29:11

It's a Day of Destiny

It's a day of destiny,
A time to begin again.
All your past regrets and sin
Have been crucified with Him.

It's a day of destiny,
The choice is yours today.
A path of new tomorrows,
Will open when you pray.

The path is not always easy
The way is narrow and hard,
But God's love will guide you,
And strengthen your failing heart.

If you want a life that is meaningful,
That fulfills your heart's desire,
Look no further than the cross of Christ,
Where He exchanged His life for ours.

Because you are deeply loved by my Father, God still has a purpose and plan for your life. Even when your own decisions have taken you far away from the path of life He originally planned, He stands ready to mend your broken heart and restore your broken dreams. With each breath of life that the Father gives you, I know that He will guide you and guard you ever so closely in the very palm of His hand.

The plan that God is unfolding in your life and in mine is glorious indeed. For this plan is not something that you and I would have thought of together. It is not something that we could have worked out on our own.[49] God's ways are so much more wonderful than we could ever think or imagine.[50]

Because of the grace God has given you, you can teach others that God's way is best. By sharing with others what you have learned, many who followed the way of darkness will turn back to God, and many children just like me will have the chance to live the life God has planned for them since the beginning of time.

God would never have created me if He did not have a special plan for my life, and your life too. And I know in my heart that even though my life on Earth can never be, I can still bring glory and honor to my Father in heaven. He has said that everything that "happens to us is working for our good if we love God and are fitting into His plans,"[51] and my heavenly Father is always true to His Word.

And remember Mom, my life, and your life, too, is no longer about the past. It is about the future. Use my story to tell others that God's ways are always best, and that life is truly sacred both in heaven and on Earth. Just tell other Moms to love their children and give them the life that God has planned for them since the beginning of time.

Talk

1. How does an abortion affect the promises and plans God originally planned for you and your child?

_____

_____

_____

_____

_____

_____

2. God is the author of forgiveness. How can coming to God with a broken and contrite heart help to build bridges of hope, restoration, and life?

_____

_____

_____

_____

_____

Chapter 10

The Secret Places of a Wounded Heart

Through the Eyes of Grace

I now see my mother through the eyes

of my Father's love and grace.

From a loving daughter's heart,

Pamela Jean

Broken, Mended, and *New* Again

She is not broken anymore.
She is stronger, wiser,
and more beautiful than before
because God took her broken pieces
and made her new again.[52]

A *Heart* Rescued for Life

"The Lord is close to those whose hearts are breaking;
He rescues those who are humbly sorry for their sins."
Psalm 34:18

God knows everything about you, yet He loves you still. He knows all about your broken heart, and He knows, too, that you desire to love Him and to live for Him for the rest of your life.

I know that God can give back to you the joy of your salvation. Even though you have experienced sadness and loss, the light of God's presence can help you see the wonderful life God still has in store for you. Your heart has been rescued for life![53]

In heaven I have learned from my Father that there is a special place in God's heart for those who come to Him with a broken and contrite heart. The deep sorrow that you have felt in your heart can be turned into an indescribable joy. He alone can give you a new start and help you to forget the past and to look forward to the life He has planned for you.

Even when you are in the deepest and darkest places of your life, I know my Father understands and will never leave your side. Take care to not let the enemy take away the beautiful joy and love He is wanting to give you now. I know that when my Father touches a life, He makes everything new, and I can see His work in you.

When you truly understand that God loves you, you will be able to face life with courage, strength, and dignity. He can fill your heart with a new song and give you lips that will declare His praise.[54] He loves you, Mom, and I love you too. Your joy and happiness will shine forth from your heart like a brilliant light for all to see. I hope to see you soon, but until that time, I will wait with joy and gladness as I watch from heaven's door.

Life Talk

1. When you give your heart to the Lord, you have a Father who will never leave you or forsake you. How can a true understanding of your Father's love help you face life with "courage, strength, and dignity?"

_____

_____

_____

_____

_____

2. In the secret places of your heart, is there a special prayer that you would like to share with your heavenly Father?

_____

_____

_____

_____

_____

Chapter 11

A Sweet Goodbye

I Will *Always* Wonder

Even as I say goodbye,

I will always wonder,

"Who was I supposed to be?"

All my love,

Pamela Jean

In God's *Perfect* Time

I never got to hold your hand,
Walk on beaches and feel the sand,
Or look at the sky on a starry night
And see the creation God has planned.

But one day, in God's own perfect time,
I'll see you face to face.
And then with all the love in my heart,
I'll hold your hand in mine.

We'll talk of things that might have been
and how things still can be.
We'll joyfully sing around God's throne,
The Father, you, and me.

Pamela Jean

Well, Mom, it's time for me to say goodbye. I leave you in the hands of the Father of Life himself. And even now, I can see through the eyes of faith that God will use you in incredible ways for His kingdom and glory. I know that He will give you His own sweet Spirit to guide and direct you all the days of your life. I know that you will always be filled to overflowing with the incomparible love of our Father.

I know I'll see you soon, for I am looking at the clocks of heaven which always chime on the heartbeat of our Father's love. A minute in heaven can almost seem like forever on Earth, but remember, "a day or a thousand years from now is like tomorrow to the Lord."[55]

So please, Mom, never forget that you have a daughter in heaven who loves you with all of her heart. And remember always, I am forever loved, forever known, and forever watching you from the throne room of God's grace. For while we cannot undo the past, God can give you everything you need on Earth to live a life that can give our Father great glory and joy from this time forward.[56] Keep running the race God has set before you.[57] I will be watching and cheering you on until you reach the finish line!

I love you, Mom, and my Father loves you too. I am so glad that God gave me you. Keep me always in your heart. I'll keep waiting and watching for that special day when we will meet at last, face to face forever more.

With all my love,
Your daughter in heaven,

Pamela Jean

 Talk

1. Has the story of Pamela Jean helped you to understand the true value and worth of the unborn child?

_____

_____

_____

_____

_____

2. What is the most significant lesson you will take away from this book regarding the sanctity of life?

_____

_____

_____

_____

_____

3. How can you be a voice for children who cannot speak for themselves?

_____

_____

_____

_____

_____

_____

4. In your own life, how will you use your own understanding of the sanctity of life to make wise and godly decisions for the glory of God and His kingdom?

_____

_____

_____

_____

_____

_____

Choices of Destiny

Miracles at the Crossroads of Life

Some Miracles Were *Never* Planned

Sanctuary or Tomb

A mother conceived, in her eyes, not planned,

Only through faith's eyes could she see,

That God was working for His Glory;

He was reaching out His Hand.

For in this story

the Child grew up,

And we know today,

He became the Son of Man.

If you conceived and have a child in heaven

Who was never given birth,

God stands ready to forgive you,

But reminds you, your child has worth.

But if you now have life

Bursting forth within your womb,

May your child find a sanctuary,

And not a waiting tomb.

Endnotes

1 New American Bible (Revised Edition) NABRE

2 Ps. 139:14, King James Version (KJV)

3 cf. Matt. 10:30, Luke 12:7

4 cf. Jer. 1:5

5 cf. Jer. 1:5

6 cf. Ps. 139:13-16

7 cf. Rev. 21:4

8 cf. Neh. 8:10

9 1 Cor. 2:9

10 cf. 1 Cor. 2:9

11 cf. Rev. 21:23

12 cf. 2 Cor. 5:1, Heb. 13:14

13 cf. Rev. 21:21

14 Zech. 8:5

15 cf. Phil. 3:13

16 cf. 1 Cor. 13:4-13

17 cf. Gal. 5:22

18 cf. Ps. 23:1-3

19 Ps. 23:3

20 cf. John 14:2-3

21 cf. Jer. 29:11

22 cf. Rom. 8:28

23 cf. 1 Cor. 15:55-57

24 cf. Rom. 8:28

25 cf. Rev. 2:4

26 cf. Ps. 51:17

27 cf. 2 Cor. 5:17

28 cf. Jer. 29:11

29 cf. Matt. 28:20

30 Some content taken from *The Atonement Child* by Francine Rivers. Copyright © (2012). Used by permission of Tyndale House Publishers, Inc. All rights reserved.

31 cf. 2 Cor. 5:17

32 cf. Heb.12:1, King James Version (KJV)

33 cf. Isa. 61:3

34 cf. Heb. 12:1, King James Version (KJV)

35 cf. John 10:10

36 cf. 2 Cor. 5:17

37 cf. Matt. 6:19-20, Phil. 3:13-14

38 cf. Neh. 8:10, Ps.28:7

39 cf. Matt. 5:14

40 cf. Phil. 4:7

41 cf. Ps. 51:10

42 cf. Isa.1:18

43 cf. Ezek. 36:26

44 cf. Joel 2:25

45 Ps. 103:5

46 cf. Isa. 61:3, New International Version (NIV)

47 cf. 2 Pet. 3:18, Deut. 32:10, Ps.17:8, Zech. 2:8

48 cf. Rev. 3:5

49 cf. Isa. 55:8-9

50 cf. Eph. 3:20-21

51 Rom. 8:28

52 The Word for the Day: Hope in Jesus http://thewordforth-eday.tumblr.com/post/122828073202/job-1711-my-days-are-over-my-hopes-have

53 cf. John 8:12

54 cf. Ps. 40:3

55 2 Pet. 3:8

56 cf. Phil. 3:13-14

57 cf. Heb. 12:1-2, Phil. 3:14, 1 Cor. 9:24-27, 2 Tim. 4:7-8

Connecting with the Author
Let's Connect for Life

"Be fearless in your stand for truth and honesty.
And may God use you to defend the innocent."
2 Chronicles 19:11

Debra D. Watkins, M.Ed., PhD
P.O. Box 521
Bellville, TX 77418

MyPamelaJean@gmail.com
www.MyNameIsPamelaJean.com
Like us on Facebook

Made in the USA
Monee, IL
14 April 2021